WORLD SERIES SCRAPBOOK

by JAMES PRELLER

SCHOLASTIC INC.
New York   Toronto   London   Auckland   Sydney
Mexico City   New Delhi   Hong Kong   Buenos Aires

For my father,
who had the good sense to bring us to the 5th
and final game of the 1969 World Series.
I was eight and I still remember.
—J.P.

COVER PHOTO CREDITS
Schilling: Jeff Zelevansky/ICON SMI. **Pujols:** Jason Wise/ICON SMI. **Jeter:** Jeff Zelevansky/ICON SMI.
Beckett: Dilip Vishwanat/ICON SMI. **Back cover:** J.B. Forbes/ICON SMI.

No part of this publication may be reproduced, stored in a retrieval system, or transmitted in any form or by any means, electronic, mechanical, photocopying, recording, or otherwise, without written permission of the publisher. For information regarding permission, write to Scholastic Inc., Attention: Permissions Department, 557 Broadway, New York, NY 10012.

ISBN 0-439-80066-8

Copyright © 2005 by James Preller
All rights reserved.
Published by Scholastic Inc.

SCHOLASTIC and associated logos are trademarks and/or registered trademarks of Scholastic Inc.

12 11 10 9 8 7 6 5 4 3 2 1   5 6 7 8 9 10 / 0

Printed in the U.S.A.
First printing, September 2005
Book design by Michael Malone

MRS. TURNER

YOU NEVER KNOW WHO IS GOING TO COME UP **BIG.**

Every World Series, players help their teams win with dramatic home runs, great pitching performances, clutch hits, and diving catches. These heroes range from proven superstars to lesser-known role players.

In fact, we're never sure who the next hero will be—and that's half the fun. Because in the World Series, any player might be given the opportunity to come up big.

For the purposes of this book, we've shined a light on recent World Series heroes from the post-strike era (1995 to the present). Catch a rising star!

JOSH BECKETT
PITCHER

JOSH BECKETT
BATS RIGHT, THROWS RIGHT
HEIGHT 6' 4", WEIGHT 190 LB.
BORN 5/15/80 IN SPRING, TX

WORLD SERIES RECORD-HOLDERS
ERA (20 IP, minimum)

		ERA	IP
1.	Jack Billingham	0.36	25.1
2.	Harry Brecheen	0.83	32.2
3.	Claude Osteen	0.86	21.0
4.	Babe Ruth	0.87	31.0
5.	Sherry Smith	0.89	30.1
6.	Sandy Koufax	0.95	57.0
7.	Christy Mathewson	0.97	101.2
8.	Hippo Vaughn	1.00	127.0
9.	Monte Pearson	1.01	35.2
10.	Mariano Rivera	1.16	31.0

A Dream Come True

It is every baseball-loving boy's dream. To take the mound in a stadium filled to overflowing with wild, raucous fans. Let's say 55,773 screaming fans, to be exact. And since it's just a dream we're talking about, why not make it the most famous stadium of them all: Yankee Stadium, home of baseball's most feared franchise, the Bronx Bombers.

> **WHEN JOSH BECKETT** took the mound to start Game Six of the 2003 World Series, his career record stood at a modest 17 wins and 17 losses. He had never thrown a shutout in the big leagues. But at the end of two hours and fifty-seven minutes, he was a World Series hero.

And in this dream (since we're only dreaming, you see), you are not going to get knocked around by opposing hitters, are you? No, you are going to throw blistering fastballs right by the best sluggers in the game. You are going to buckle their knees with big overhand curveballs. And your changeup, coming after that 97 MPH heater? Well, it's just not fair, but it sure is fun.

For Josh Beckett, age 23, it wasn't a fantasy. It was the fulfillment of a promise. He took the mound for Game Six without a trace of self-doubt and threw a gem for the ages. Come the 9th inning, with three outs to go, manager Jack McKeon went against conventional wisdom. He wasn't going to trust this game—this Series, this Dream—to some guy in the bullpen. So Jack sent Josh out there, like David with his slingshot, to finish off Goliath right then and there. Beckett got Bernie Williams to fly to left. Hideki Matsui, too. Then Jorge Posada hit a slow roller down the first base line that Josh fielded himself. He tagged out Posada, and the game was over: Marlins 2, Yankees 0. The stadium stands fell silent. Then a crowd of Marlins rushed to the mound. They lifted Josh Beckett onto their shoulders. He looked around, jubilant, triumphant. He wasn't dreaming.

BECKETT 2003 SERIES STATS

G	ERA	W-L	IP	H	ER	BB	SO
2	1.10	1-1	16.1	8	2	5	19

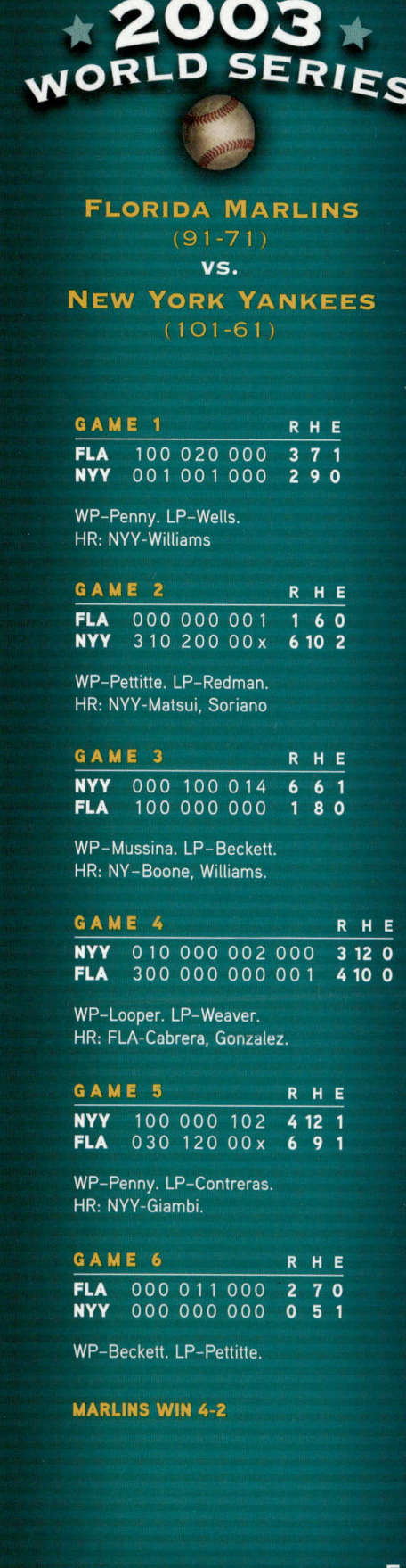

2003 WORLD SERIES

FLORIDA MARLINS
(91-71)
vs.
NEW YORK YANKEES
(101-61)

GAME 1
		R	H	E
FLA	100 020 000	3	7	1
NYY	001 001 000	2	9	0

WP–Penny. LP–Wells.
HR: NYY–Williams

GAME 2
		R	H	E
FLA	000 000 001	1	6	0
NYY	310 200 00x	6	10	2

WP–Pettitte. LP–Redman.
HR: NYY–Matsui, Soriano

GAME 3
		R	H	E
NYY	000 100 014	6	6	1
FLA	100 000 000	1	8	0

WP–Mussina. LP–Beckett.
HR: NY–Boone, Williams.

GAME 4
		R	H	E
NYY	010 000 002 000	3	12	0
FLA	300 000 000 001	4	10	0

WP–Looper. LP–Weaver.
HR: FLA–Cabrera, Gonzalez.

GAME 5
		R	H	E
NYY	100 000 102	4	12	1
FLA	030 120 00x	6	9	1

WP–Penny. LP–Contreras.
HR: NYY–Giambi.

GAME 6
		R	H	E
FLA	000 011 000	2	7	0
NYY	000 000 000	0	5	1

WP–Beckett. LP–Pettitte.

MARLINS WIN 4-2

TROY GLAUS
THIRD BASE

TROY EDWARD GLAUS
BATS RIGHT, THROWS RIGHT
HEIGHT 6' 5", WEIGHT 245 LB.
BORN 8/3/76 IN NEWPORT BEACH, CA

POSTSEASON RECORD-HOLDERS
Slugging Percentage

		SLG	PA
1.	Carlos Beltran	1.022	56
2.	**Troy Glaus**	.819	82
3.	Todd Walker	.767	46
4.	Babe Ruth	.744	167
5.	Juan Gonzalez	.742	66
6.	Lou Gehrig	.731	150
7.	Willie Aikens	.725	49
8.	Hank Aaron	.710	74
9.	Bobby Brown	.707	46
10.	Rusty Staub	.683	46

MAN ON FIRE

Troy Glaus, the former Anaheim Angels' slugging third baseman, entered the 2002 season with high hopes. After all, in 2001 he smacked more than 40 homers for the second season in a row. Things could only get better, right? Well, maybe not at first. Despite his team's success, Troy struggled through much of the regular season. In June and July, he batted a terrible .198, losing his power stroke for weeks at a time. Still, Troy showed a knack for coming up with clutch hits.

IT WAS DECIDED: THE ANGELS were not going to let Barry Bonds beat them. So they walked Barry a record-setting thirteen times. A good strategy? Take a gander at what happened when the Angels pitched to him. The guy mashed.

BONDS 2002 SERIES STATS

AB	R	H	2B	3B	HR	RBI	BB	BA	OBP	SLG
17	8	8	2	0	4	6	13	.471	.700	1.29

But for the Angels to go anywhere in the playoffs, manager Mike Scioscia knew they needed more consistency from Troy's big bat. And, boy, did he deliver. Troy caught fire and stayed hot. In the postseason, he hit .344 overall and banged out seven home runs (one short of the record set by—who else?—Barry Bonds).

Troy saved his best for when it counted most, hitting .385 with 8 RBIs in a wild and wooly rumpus called the 2002 World Series. A World Series that will be remembered for one of the greatest comebacks in series history. Up three games to two, the Giants held a commanding 5-0 lead in Game Six as they entered the bottom half of the 7th inning. In the 8th, the Giants were clinging to a 5-4 lead when Troy Glaus stepped to the plate with two runners on base. The burly third baseman lined a shot deep to the left-center gap to drive in two and complete the comeback. The Angels would live to play, and win, a seventh game.

John Cordes/ICON SMI

GLAUS 2002 SERIES STATS

AB	R	H	2B	3B	HR	RBI	BB	BA	OBP	SLG	SB
22	6	9	2	1	2	2	3	.409	.480	.864	0

★ 2002 ★
WORLD SERIES

ANAHEIM ANGELS
(99-63)
vs.
SAN FRANCISCO GIANTS
(95-66)

GAME 1   R H E
SFG   100 000 102   4 12 1
ANA   030 120 00x   6 9 1

WP–Schmidt. LP–Washburn.
HR: SFG–Bonds, Sanders, Snow;
ANA–Glaus (2).

GAME 2   R H E
SFG   041 040 001   10 12 1
ANA   520 011 02x   11 16 1

WP–Fr. Rodriguez. LP–Fe. Rodriguez.
HR: SFG–Sanders, Bell, Kent, Bonds;
ANA–Salmon (2).

GAME 3   R H E
ANA   004 401 010   10 16 1
SFG   100 030 000   4 6 2

WP–Ortiz. LP–Hernandez.
HR: SFG–Aurilia, Bonds.

GAME 4   R H E
ANA   012 000 000   3 10 1
SFG   000 030 01x   4 12 1

WP–Worrell. LP–Fr. Rodriguez.
HR: ANA–Glaus. SV–Nen

GAME 5   R H E
ANA   000 031 000   4 10 2
SFG   330 002 44x   16 16 0

WP–Zerbe. LP–Washburn.
HR: SFG–Kent (2), Aurilia.

GAME 6   R H E
SFG   000 031 000   5 8 1
ANA   000 000 33x   6 10 1

WP–Donnelly. LP–Worrell.
HR: SFG–Dunston, Bonds;
ANA–Spiezio, Erstad.

GAME 7   R H E
SFG   010 000 000   1 6 0
ANA   013 000 00x   4 5 0

WP–Lackey. LP–Hernandez.

ANGELS WIN 4-3

TOM GLAVINE
PITCHER

THOMAS MICHAEL GLAVINE
BATS LEFT, THROWS LEFT
HEIGHT 6' 1", WEIGHT 190 LB.
BORN 3/25/66 IN CONCORD, MA

POSTSEASON RECORD-HOLDERS
Most innings pitched

1.	John Smoltz	199.2
2.	**Tom Glavine**	**194.0**
3.	Greg Maddux	190.0
4.	Andy Pettitte	186.2
5.	Roger Clemens	180.2
6.	Whitey Ford	146.0
7.	Dave Stewart	133.0
8.	Catfish Hunter	132.1
9.	Orel Hershiser	132.0
10.	Jim Palmer	124.1

Nearly Perfect

Since 1991, the Atlanta Braves have been in the postseason thirteen consecutive years (skipping the strike-shortened 1994 season). That's the good news. The bad news is that during that span the Braves won the World Series exactly once, back in 1995 against the Cleveland Indians. Every other year ended with a loss.

> **WHEN YOU MAKE A LIST** of the fiercest hitting teams to never win the World Series, consider the 1995 Cleveland Indians: Kenny Lofton, Omar Vizquel, Carlos Baerga, Albert Belle, Eddie Murray, Manny Ramirez, Jim Thome, Sandy Alomar, and Paul Sorrentino. Together those nine represent a staggering 43 All-Star appearances! For opposing pitchers, the torture never stopped.

Credit for that World Series Championship goes to pitching. The Braves staff included starters Greg Maddux, Steve Avery, and John Smoltz. But in this World Series, the best of the bunch was a soft-tossing, hockey-loving southpaw named Tom Glavine. Twice manager Bobby Cox sent Tom out to the hill, and both times he shut down one of baseball's toughest lineups. Never a power pitcher, Tom relied on pinpoint control and a great changeup to offset a ferocious Tribe attack.

In one of the greatest pitching performances of World Series history, Tom Glavine was nearly perfect in Game Six. He would have to be. For the Braves would score one mere run on a solo dinger by David Justice. Through the first five innings, Tom didn't surrender a hit. He pitched ever-so-carefully to Albert Belle, walking the dangerous cleanup hitter twice. Tom retired everybody else who stepped to the plate. Thoughts of an historic no-hitter came to an end when back-up catcher Tony Pena blooped a single to start the sixth inning. That was all the Indians could scratch out. After giving up only one hit and three walks, Tom ended the day by bringing home the MVP Award and a World Series ring.

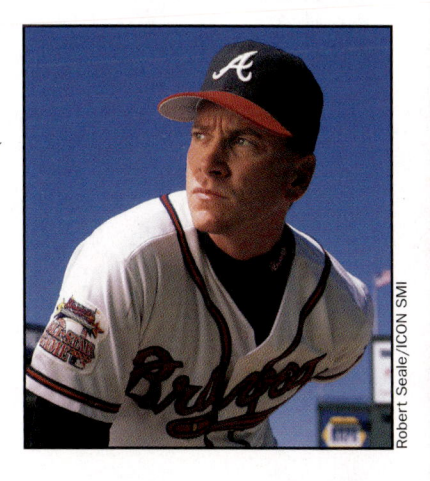

GLAVINE 1995 SERIES STATS

G	ERA	W-L	IP	H	ER	BB	SO
2	1.29	2-0	14.0	4	2	6	11

1995 WORLD SERIES

ATLANTA BRAVES
(90-54)
vs.
CLEVELAND INDIANS
(100-44)

GAME 1
```
              R  H  E
CLE 100 000 001   2  2  0
ATL 010 000 20x   3  3  2
```
WP-Maddux. LP-Hershiser.
HR: ATL-McGriff.

GAME 2
```
              R  H  E
CLE 020 000 100   3  6  2
ATL 002 002 00x   4  8  2
```
WP-Glavine. LP-Martinez.
HR: CLE-Murray; ATL-Lopez.

GAME 3
```
              R   H  E
ATL 100 001 130 00   6  12  1
CLE 202 000 110 01   7  12  2
```
WP-Mesa. LP-Pena.
HR: ATL-McGriff, Klesko.

GAME 4
```
              R  H  E
ATL 000 001 301   5 11  1
CLE 000 001 001   2  6  0
```
WP-Avery. LP-Hill.
HR: ATL-Klesko; CLE-Belle, Ramirez.

GAME 5
```
              R  H  E
ATL 000 110 002   4  7  0
CLE 200 002 01x   5  8  1
```
WP-Hershiser. LP-Maddux.
HR: ATL-Polonia, Klesko;
CLE-Belle, Thome.

GAME 6
```
              R  H  E
CLE 000 000 000   0  1  1
ATL 000 001 00x   1  6  0
```
WP-Glavine. LP-Poole.
HR: ATL-Justice.

BRAVES WIN 4-2

DEREK JETER
SHORTSTOP

DEREK SANDERSON JETER
BATS: RIGHT, THROWS: RIGHT
HEIGHT: 6' 3", WEIGHT: 175 LB.
BORN: 6/26/74 IN PEQUANNOCK, NJ

POSTSEASON RECORD HOLDERS
Most games played

1.	Yogi Berra	150
2.	Mickey Mantle	130
3.	Bernie Williams	115
4.	David Justice	112
5.	**Derek Jeter**	**110**
6.	Reggie Jackson	109
7.	Elston Howard	108
8.	Hank Bauer	106
	Gil McDougald	106
10.	Phil Rizzuto	104

Steady Performer

A star for the New York Yankees since 1996, shortstop Derek Jeter has played in a lot of big games. Across ten seasons, he's appeared in nine Division Series, seven League Championship Series, and six World Series—a total of 110 postseason games. And counting.

Some of that is luck—he hasn't been toiling in Tampa Bay or Milwaukee. No, Derek earns $20 million a year to play spectacularly well for George Steinbrenner's pinstriped sluggers. The other thing, the part you can't ever forget, is that Mr. Jeter has earned a lot of those opportunities. In crunch time, he's made a lot of big plays. He's crushed a bunch of baseballs along the way.

WHILE SOME EXPERTS call Jeter "Mr. Clutch," it's more accurate to say that he's "Mr. Steady," playing at his accustomed high level even when the pressure is the greatest.

	G	AVG	OBP	SLG
Career	1,366	.315	.385	.463
Postseason	110	.306	.380	.456

Derek was named MVP of the 2000 World Series for his outstanding overall play. But one at-bat stands out. Though the Yankees won the series four games to one, it was an extraordinary, hard-fought series. Each game was a nail-biter, where one play could turn the tide. After going up two games to none, the Yankees lost Game Three to the Mets. It felt as if momentum may have turned for the team from Flushing. Game Four at Shea was going to be pivotal. Derek Jeter led off against Mets hurler, Bobby Jones. Mets catcher Mike Piazza never touched the first pitch. Because Jeter swung and deposited it over the left field wall. For the fourth time in his career, Derek Jeter would be earning a World Series ring.

David Seelig/ICON SMI

JETER 2000 SERIES STATS

AB	R	H	2B	3B	HR	RBI	BB	BA	OBP	SLG	SB
22	6	9	2	1	2	2	3	.409	.480	.864	0

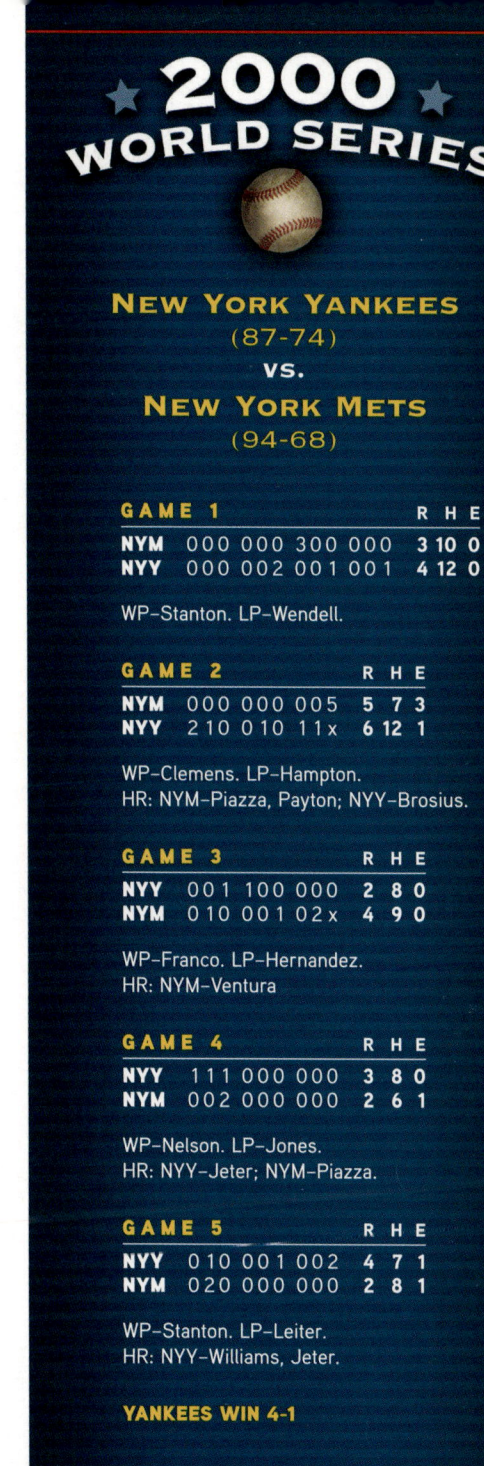

2000 WORLD SERIES

NEW YORK YANKEES
(87-74)
vs.
NEW YORK METS
(94-68)

GAME 1
		R	H	E
NYM	000 000 300 000	3	10	0
NYY	000 002 001 001	4	12	0

WP–Stanton. LP–Wendell.

GAME 2
		R	H	E
NYM	000 000 005	5	7	3
NYY	210 010 11x	6	12	1

WP–Clemens. LP–Hampton.
HR: NYM–Piazza, Payton; NYY–Brosius.

GAME 3
		R	H	E
NYY	001 100 000	2	8	0
NYM	010 001 02x	4	9	0

WP–Franco. LP–Hernandez.
HR: NYM–Ventura.

GAME 4
		R	H	E
NYY	111 000 000	3	8	0
NYM	002 000 000	2	6	1

WP–Nelson. LP–Jones.
HR: NYY–Jeter; NYM–Piazza.

GAME 5
		R	H	E
NYY	010 001 002	4	7	1
NYM	020 000 000	2	8	1

WP–Stanton. LP–Leiter.
HR: NYY–Williams, Jeter.

YANKEES WIN 4-1

RANDY JOHNSON
PITCHER

RANDALL DAVID JOHNSON
BATS RIGHT, THROWS LEFT
HEIGHT 6' 10", WEIGHT 225 LB.
BORN 9/10/63 IN WALNUT CREEK, CA

WORLD SERIES
RECORD-HOLDERS
Most Wins in a World Series

Babe Adams	3	1909 WS
Harry Brecheen	3	1946 WS
Lew Burdette	3	1957 WS
Jack Coombs	3	1910 WS
Stan Coveleski	3	1920 WS
Bill Dineen	3	1903 WS
Red Faber	3	1917 WS
Bob Gibson	3	1967 WS
Randy Johnson	**3**	**2001 WS**
Mickey Lolich	3	1968 WS
Christy Mathewson	3	1905 WS
Deacon Phillippe	3	1903 WS
Joe Wood	3	1912 WS

John McDonough/ICON SMI

THE BIG UNIT

It's a familiar tale. Often in baseball we'll watch as a player puts together a wonderful career. All-Star games, major awards, sneaker endorsements, the works. But then the experts on ESPN will inform us that his career, though great, will never be complete until he plays on a World Series winner.

Maybe that's not fair. After all, baseball is a team game. No single player can carry an entire roster on his back to a world championship. But sometimes guys will try. Please consider Exhibit A: left-hander Randy Johnson in the year 2001, star pitcher for the Diamondbacks. Ringless. For a while there, anyway.

Entering the 2005 season, Randy has already enjoyed a Hall of Fame career. He's won 246 games, he's a ten-time All-Star, a five-time Cy Young Award winner, and he ranks third on the all-time strikeout list with 4,161. Not to mention that his slider is filthy.

In the 2001 World Series, Randy fired a masterful three-hit shutout in Game Two, whiffing 11 hapless Yankees along the way. He got the start again in Game Six, and this time Randy coasted to a 15-2 victory. The very next day, in Game Seven, Randy came on in relief with the Diamondbacks trailing 2-1. Randy did the job again, four up, four down, keeping the game close. The stage was set for the Snakes' amazing comeback in the bottom of the 9th—and a third World Series victory for Randy Johnson!

AFTER THE 2004 SEASON ENDED in despair for the Yankees, management decided that the Yanks needed a frontline pitcher. A twirler who could flat-out dominate. Somebody who could carry a team to victory in the postseason. Is it any wonder they targeted Randy Johnson? Just look at RJ's career postseason record vs. the Men in Pinstripes:

POSTSEASON RECORD VS. YANKEES

G	GS	ERA	W-L	IP	H	ER	BB	SO
5	3	1.65	5-0	27.1	14	5	9	35

JOHNSON 2001 SERIES STATS

G	ERA	W-L	IP	H	ER	BB	SO
3	1.04	3-0	17.1	9	2	3	19

Chuck Solomon/ICON SMI

2001 WORLD SERIES

ARIZONA DIAMONDBACKS
(92-70)
vs.
NEW YORK YANKEES
(95-65)

GAME 1 R H E
NYY 100 000 000 1 3 2
ARI 104 400 00x 9 10 0

WP-Schilling. LP-Mussina.
HR: ARI-Counsell, Gonzalez.

GAME 2 R H E
NYY 000 000 000 0 3 0
ARI 010 000 30x 4 5 0

WP-Johnson. LP-Pettitte.
HR: ARI-Williams.

GAME 3 R H E
ARI 000 100 000 1 3 3
NYY 010 001 00x 2 7 1

WP-Clemens. LP-Anderson.
HR: NYY-Posada.

GAME 4 R H E
ARI 000 100 020 0 3 6 0
NYY 001 000 002 1 4 7 0

WP-Rivera. LP-Kim.
HR: ARI-Grace;
NYY-Jeter, Martinez, Spencer.

GAME 5 R H E
ARI 000 020 000 000 2 8 0
NYY 000 000 002 001 3 9 1

WP-Hitchcock. LP-Lopez.
HR: ARI-Finley, Barajas; NYY-Brosius.

GAME 6 R H E
NYY 000 002 000 2 7 1
ARI 138 300 00x 15 22 0

WP-Johnson. LP-Pettitte.

GAME 7 R H E
NYY 000 000 110 2 6 3
ARI 000 001 002 3 11 0

WP-Johnson. LP-Rivera.
HR: NYY-Soriano.

DIAMONDBACKS WIN 4-3

ALBERT PUJOLS
FIRST BASE

JOSE ALBERTO PUJOLS
BATS RIGHT, THROWS RIGHT
HEIGHT 6' 3", WEIGHT 210 LB.
BORN 1/16/80 IN SANTO DOMINGO, D.R.

POSTSEASON RECORD HOLDERS
Total bases, single series

		TB	SERIES
1.	Hideki Matsui	28	2004 ALCS
	Albert Pujols	**28**	**2004 NLCS**
3.	Reggie Jackson	25	1977 WS
	Willie Stargell	25	1979 WS
5.	Carlos Beltran	24	2004 NLDS2
	Lou Brock	24	1968 WS
	Will Clark	24	1989 NLCS
	Ken Griffey	24	1995 ALDS2
	Javy Lopez	24	1996 NLCS
	Paull Molitor	24	1993 WS
	Duke Snider	24	1952 WS

THE MACHINE

It is hard to shine when your team is getting swept in the World Series, four games to none. When your team is losing by a cumulative score of 24-12, it's hard to stand out as one of the game's greatest players. Unless you are Albert Pujols, and you possess one of the sweetest swings in baseball. Then you shine anywhere, anytime.

NO FOOLING. Albert features such outstanding balance in the batter's box, that he rarely seems fooled at the plate. He can drive the ball to all fields with power. He always seems to put a good swing on the ball. Very simply, pitchers don't make Albert look bad. It's the reverse that's true.

Albert entered the 2004 World Series as the best young hitter in baseball. He's sometimes called "The Machine" because that's how it seems; he's automatic, beyond human, without discernible flaws. He just steps into the box and strokes doubles. Albert has played four full seasons of Major League Baseball for the Redbirds. During that period, well, just look at the numbers (p.16).

In 2004, "Phat Albert" had almost as many home runs (46) as strikeouts (52). That's crazy good. He led the Cards to the best record in baseball, then got even better in the postseason. He warmed up by smacking two bombs off the Dodgers in the NLDS. He was a monster in the NLCS, a brutal seven-game series against the Houston Astros. Albert went 14 for 28 with 4 homers, 9 RBIs, a .500 batting average with a 1.000 slugging percentage!

In the 2004 World Series, Albert remained his steady, spectacular, superstar self. Unfortunately, the Cards two other big sluggers—Jim Edmunds and Scott Rolen—picked an awful time to slump, going 1-30 in the series. The Cards went down 4-0 to a Red Sox team that seemed destined to win it all. But Albert Pujols made sure it wasn't without a fight.

PUJOLS 2004 SERIES STATS

AB	R	H	2B	3B	HR	RBI	BB	BA	OBP	SLG	SB
15	1	5	2	0	0	0	1	.333	.412	.467	0

2004 WORLD SERIES

BOSTON RED SOX
(98-64)
vs.
ST. LOUIS CARDINALS
(105-57)

GAME 1   R   H   E
STL 011 302 020   9 11   1
BOS 403 000 22x   11 13   4

WP-Foulke. LP-Tavarez.
HR: STL–Walker; BOS–Ortiz, Bellhorn.

GAME 2   R   H   E
STL 000 100 010   2   5   0
BOS 200 202 00x   6   8   4

WP-Schilling. LP-Morris.

GAME 3   R   H   E
BOS 100 120 000   4   9   0
STL 000 000 001   1   4   0

WP-Martinez. LP-Suppan.
HR: BOS–Ramirez; STL–Walker.

GAME 4   R   H   E
BOS 102 000 000   3   9   0
STL 000 000 000   0   4   0

WP-Lowe. LP-Marquis.
HR: BOS–Damon.

RED SOX WIN 4-0

Future Hall-of-Famer

Albert Pujols is eerily consistent, as dependable as the rising sun. Rookie of the Year in 2001, a two-time runner-up for the NL MVP Award (2002, 2003), a batting crown champion (2003), first in runs scored in consecutive seasons (2003, 2004), and—while we're at it—first in extra-base hits those same two years (2003, 2004). That's not a machine, folks, that's a monster. If you collect baseball cards, and own his Rookie Card, keep it. Because someday it'll be worth something.

YR	AVG	OBP	SLG	AB	2B	HR	RBI	BB	K
2001	.329	.403	.610	590	47	37	130	69	93
2002	.314	.394	.561	590	40	34	127	72	69
2003	.359	.439	.667	591	51	43	124	79	65
2004	.331	.415	.657	592	51	46	123	84	52
Career	.333	.415	.624	2363	189	160	504	304	279

Larry Goren/ICON SMI

17

EDGAR
RENTERIA
SHORTSTOP

EDGAR ENRIQUE RENTERIA
BATS RIGHT, THROWS RIGHT
HEIGHT 6' 1", WEIGHT 172 LB.
BORN 8/7/75 IN BARRANQUILLA, COLOMBIA

ONE SWING OF THE BAT

Have you ever imagined yourself up at the plate in a clutch situation? With all the world watching? If you've played any baseball, the answer is probably yes. Your daydream probably went something like this:

Baseball Announcer in the Sky: "Welcome, ladies and gentleman! What a beautiful day for baseball! Here we are at the 7th Game of the World Series. The score is tied, and we're in extra innings! Runners are at second and third, two outs. Now up at the plate, it's (enter your name here). Here comes the pitch...."

Well, here's the thing: The situation described above is EXACTLY the one faced by a young shortstop from Barranquilla, Colombia named Edgar Renteria. Of course we know him now, in 2005, as one of baseball's better shortstops. But way back in the ancient times of 1997? He was still trying to make a name for himself. And on October 26, 1997, he succeeded.

It was a Series full of stars. For the Indians: Orel Hershiser, David Justice, Jared Wright, Manny Ramirez, Jim Thome, Matt Williams, and Omar Vizquel. The Marlins featured Moises Alou, Kevin Brown, Livan Hernandez, Charles Johnson, Bobby Bonilla, Gary Sheffield, and more. But only one player delivered the hit that won it all. A young, slick-fielding shortstop who, when it mattered most, poked the ball through the infield to end the game.

THERE HAVE BEEN thirty-five 7th games in World Series history. Only five have been decided on the last swing of the bat.

1912 Boston Red Sox 3, NY Giants 2
Led by Tris Speaker and Smokey Joe Wood, the Red Stockings from Beantown score twice in the bottom of the tenth inning to win it.

1924 Washington Senators 4, NY Giants 3
Legendary Walter Johnson comes on in relief in the ninth inning and holds the Giants off through twelve. Earl McNeely's freak-hop single over third-baseman Fred Lindstrom's head wins it in the 12th inning.

1960 Pittsburgh Pirates 10, NY Yankees 9
The only walk-off home run in Game 7 World Series history. Bill Mazeroski hits a shot off Ralph Terry to end a white-knuckle slugfest in the 9th inning.

1991 Minnesota Twins 1, Atlanta Braves 0
Series MVP Jack Morris shuts out the Braves for ten brilliant innings until pinch-hitter Gene Larkin strokes a single to win it for the Twins.

1997 Florida Marlins 3, Cleveland Indians 2
Edgar Renteria smashes an RBI single up the middle in the 11th to bring the Series to a stunning close.

RENTERIA 1997 SERIES STATS

AB	R	H	2B	3B	HR	RBI	BB	BA	OBP	SLG	SB
31	3	9	2	0	0	3	3	.290	.353	.355	0

1997 WORLD SERIES

FLORIDA MARLINS
(92-70)
vs.
CLEVELAND INDIANS
(86-75)

GAME 1   R H E
CLE   100 011 010   4 11 0
FLA   001 420 00x   7 7 1

WP-Hernandez. LP-Hershiser.
HR: CLE-Ramirez, Thome;
FLA-Alou, Johnson.

GAME 2   R H E
CLE   100 032 000   6 14 0
FLA   100 000 000   1 8 0

WP-Ogea. LP-Brown. HR: CLE-Alomar.

GAME 3   R H E
FLA   101 102 207   14 16 3
CLE   200 320 004   11 10 3

WP-Cook. LP-Plunk. HR: FLA-Sheffield, Daulton, Eisenreich; CLE-Thome.

GAME 4   R H E
FLA   000 102 000   3 6 2
CLE   303 001 12x   10 15 0

WP-Wright. LP-Saunders.
HR: FLA-Alou; CLE-Ramirez, Williams.

GAME 5   R H E
FLA   020 004 011   8 15 2
CLE   013 000 003   7 9 0

WP-Hernandez. LP-Hershiser.
HR: FLA-Alou; CLE-Alomar.

GAME 6   R H E
CLE   021 010 000   4 7 0
FLA   000 010 000   1 8 0

WP-Ogea. LP-Brown. SV-Mesa

GAME 7   R H E
CLE   002 000 000 00   2 6 2
FLA   000 000 101 01   3 8 0

WP-Powell. LP-Nagy.
HR: FLA-Bonilla.

MARLINS WIN 4-3

MARIANO RIVERA
PITCHER

MARIANO RIVERA
BATS RIGHT, THROWS RIGHT
HEIGHT 6' 2", WEIGHT 170 LB.
BORN 11/29/69 IN PANAMA CITY, PANAMA

POSTSEASON RECORD-HOLDERS
Most Saves

	SV	IP
1. Mariano Rivera	32	108.2
2. Dennis Eckersley	15	36.0
3. Robb Nen	11	20.0
4. Rollie Fingers	10	57.1
5. Jason Isringhausen	9	19.2
Mark Wohlers	9	38.1
7. Rich Gossage	8	31.1
Randy Myers	8	30.2
9. Troy Percival	7	9.2
John Wetteland	7	18.2

GAME OVER

Mariano Rivera is the greatest relief pitcher in postseason history. Hey, why stop there? He may be the greatest *player* in postseason history. Of them all. That's how good he's been.

In some ways, however, he's also been the dullest. Mariano usually enters a game in exciting, pressure-filled situations and shuts the door: No more scoring for you. Amazingly, he does it primarily with one pitch, a cut fastball that eats hitters alive. They know it's coming, he knows they know it's coming, and Mariano shrugs and throws it anyway.

> **LIKE MANY RELIEVERS,** Mariano began his career as a starting pitcher. In his rookie season, 1995, Mariano started 10 games for the Yanks before moving to the bullpen—where he's stayed ever since. Good idea.

The result: A pop up, a broken bat, a pathetic two-hopper to the mound. Nobody seems to hit the ball hard, especially in the World Series.

Since 1996, Mariano Rivera has been at the heart of four Yankee World Series and six American League Championship teams. He has appeared in 70 postseason games, pitched 108.2 innings, saved 32 games, recorded 8 wins against 1 loss, and tallied a stupifying 0.75 ERA. He's struck out 85 against only 14 walks.

The Yankees sweep over the Braves almost followed a script. The New York starters pitched well, the offense scored a few runs, and then the mighty bullpen hammered in the final nail. In fact, just seeing Rivera emerge from the bullpen seemed to signal "Game over, everybody can go to bed now." He earned saves in Games One and Four. In Game Three, he worked a little harder. Mariano entered the game in the top of the ninth, score tied at five. He threw two scoreless innings until Chad Curtis ended the Braves misery with a home run. Game over.

RIVERA 1999 SERIES STATS

G	ERA	W-L	IP	H	ER	BB	SO
3	0.00	1-0	4.2	3	0	1	3

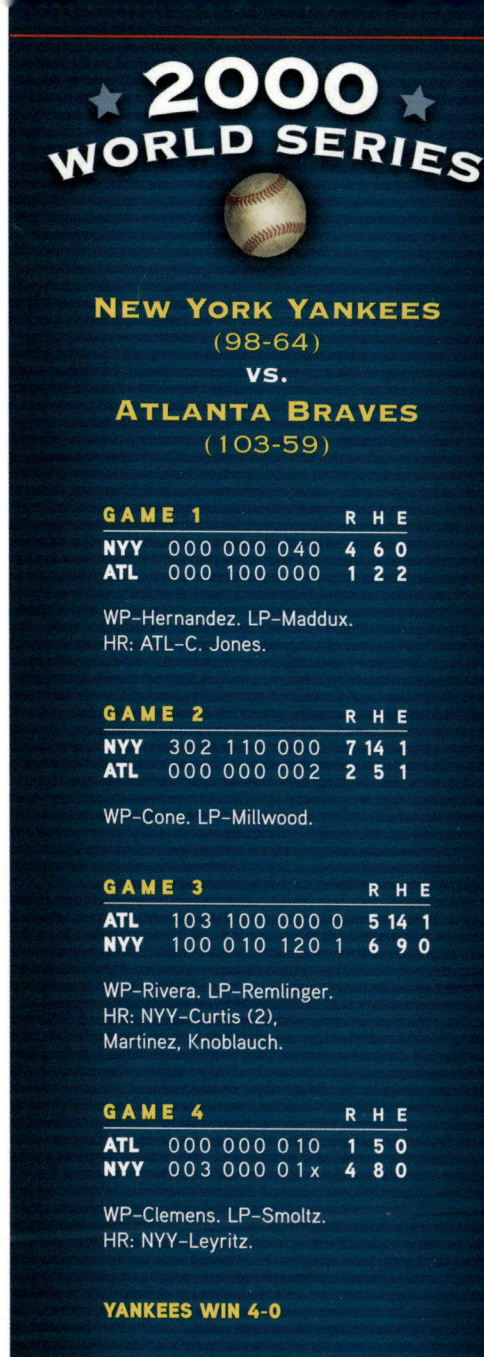

2000 WORLD SERIES

NEW YORK YANKEES
(98-64)
vs.
ATLANTA BRAVES
(103-59)

GAME 1   R H E
NYY 000 000 040   4 6 0
ATL 000 100 000   1 2 2

WP-Hernandez. LP-Maddux.
HR: ATL-C. Jones.

GAME 2   R H E
NYY 302 110 000   7 14 1
ATL 000 000 002   2 5 1

WP-Cone. LP-Millwood.

GAME 3   R H E
ATL 103 100 000 0 5 14 1
NYY 100 010 120 1 6 9 0

WP-Rivera. LP-Remlinger.
HR: NYY-Curtis (2), Martinez, Knoblauch.

GAME 4   R H E
ATL 000 000 010   1 5 0
NYY 003 000 01x   4 8 0

WP-Clemens. LP-Smoltz.
HR: NYY-Leyritz.

YANKEES WIN 4-0

IVAN RODRIGUEZ
CATCHER

IVAN RODRIGUEZ TORRES
BATS RIGHT, THROWS RIGHT
HEIGHT 5' 9", WEIGHT 205 LB.
BORN 11/27/71 IN MANATI, P.R.

Heart & Soul

During the winter before the 2003 baseball season, Ivan Rodriguez's phone didn't exactly ring off the hook. He was a free agent, yet teams were reluctant to take a risk on the aging catcher. In his previous three seasons with the Texas Rangers, back and knee injuries had kept him off the field for large chunks of time. "Pudge" was averaging only 103 games a season. Until he could prove that he was healthy, no one was willing to give him the security of a long-term contract.

> **AMONG CONTEMPORARY CATCHERS,** the debate revolves around two guys: Pudge Rodriguez and Mike Piazza. Defensively, Pudge gets the nudge. His arm is a cannon, while Piazza's is a pop gun. On offense, compare the career numbers. Edge: Piazza. Let's call it a tie!
>
> | | AB | H | HR | RBI | BA | OBP | SLG |
> |-----------|-------|-------|-----|-------|------|------|------|
> | Piazza | 5,805 | 1,829 | 378 | 1,161 | .315 | .385 | .562 |
> | Rodriguez | 6,694 | 2,051 | 250 | 1,000 | .306 | .347 | .490 |

Enter the Florida Marlins, and maybe the best $10 million ever spent. At that point, Pudge was a ten-time All-Star, an AL MVP (1999), and the winner of ten Gold Glove Awards. Marlins management surely recognized what Pudge had accomplished in the past. But more importantly, they had the vision to see what he could give them in the future—stability, leadership, heart, and soul.

Sure, Pudge put up big numbers in the postseason. His bat helped chop the Giants down to size in the NLDS. He clobbered the Cubs in the NLCS, banging out 10 RBIs and earning the MVP Award. In the World Series, Pudge was merely steady, not spectacular. But statistics only tell some of the tale. Pudge was a rock, a calming presence, a guy who steadied a young pitching staff. A guy who, in 2003, made the Marlins' management look like geniuses.

RODRIGUEZ 2003 SERIES STATS

AB	R	H	2B	3B	HR	RBI	BB	BA	OBP	SLG	SB
22	2	6	2	0	0	1	1	.273	.292	.364	0

MOST VALUABLE

Every team begins the season dreaming of the World Series. With outstanding performances in the AL and NL Championship Series over the past twenty years, these players helped lead the way.

ALCS MVP
- 2004 David Ortiz, Red Sox
- 2003 Mariano Rivera, Yankees
- 2002 Adam Kennedy, Angels
- 2001 Andy Pettitte, Yankees
- 2000 David Justice, Yankees
- 1999 Orlando Hernandez, Yankees
- 1998 David Wells, Yankees
- 1997 Marquis Grissom, Indians
- 1996 Bernie Williams, Yankees
- 1995 Orel Hershiser, Indians
- 1994 *Postseason Cancelled*
- 1993 Dave Stewart, Toronto
- 1992 Roberto Alomar, Toronto
- 1991 Kirby Puckett, Twins
- 1990 Dave Stewart, Athletics
- 1989 Rickey Henderson, Athletics
- 1988 Dennis Eckersley, Athletics
- 1987 Gary Gaetti, Twins
- 1986 Marty Barrett, Red Sox
- 1985 George Brett, Royals

NLCS MVP
- 2004 Albert Pujols, Cardinals
- **2003 Ivan Rodriguez, Marlins**
- 2002 Benito Santiago, Giants
- 2001 Craig Counsell, Diamondbacks
- 2000 Mike Hampton, Mets
- 1999 Eddie Perez, Braves
- 1998 Sterling Hitchcock, Padres
- 1997 Livan Hernandez, Marlins
- 1996 Javy Lopez, Braves
- 1995 Mike Devereaux, Braves
- 1994 *Postseason Cancelled*
- 1993 Curt Schilling, Phillies
- 1992 John Smoltz, Braves
- 1991 Steve Avery, Braves
- 1990 Rob Dibble and Randy Myers, Reds
- 1989 Will Clark, Giants
- 1988 Orel Hershiser, Dodgers
- 1987 Jeffrey Leonard, Giants
- 1986 Mike Scott, Astros
- 1985 Ozzie Smith, Cardinals

CURT SCHILLING
PITCHER

CURTIS MONTAGUE SCHILLING
BATS RIGHT, THROWS RIGHT
HEIGHT 6' 4", WEIGHT 215 LB.
BORN 11/14/66 IN ANCHORAGE, AK

WORLD SERIES RECORD-HOLDERS
Most strikeouts, single series

1.	Bob Gibson	35	1968
2.	Bob Gibson	31	1964
3.	Sandy Koufax	29	1965
4.	Bill Dineen	28	1903
5.	Bob Gibson	26	1967
	Curt Schilling	**26**	**2001**
7.	Sandy Koufax	23	1963
8.	Hal Newhouser	22	1945
	Deacon Phillippe	22	1903
10.	Mickey Lolich	21	1968
	Joe Wood	21	1912

HERO ON THE HILL

Your Honor, Ladies and Gentlemen of the Jury, we hereby submit that Curtis Montague Schilling stands before you today as the best World Series starting pitcher in baseball history. The evidence is overwhelming.

CURT IS A STUDENT of the game. He studies videos of opposing hitters' at-bats, searching for weaknesses, and then takes the mound with a detailed plan of attack.

Veteran's Stadium, Game Five, 1993 World Series: Curt hurls a complete game, five-hit shutout against the Toronto Blue Jays. *Bank One Ballpark, Game Two, 2001 World Series:* 7 IP, 3 H, 1 R, 1 BB, 8 K's; Curt's Diamondbacks defeat the New York Yankees 9-1. *Yankee Stadium, Game Four, 2001 World Series:* Curt nearly duplicates his statistical line, 7 IP, 3 H, 1 R, 1 BB, 9 K's. *Bank One Ballpark, Game Seven, 2001 World Series:* a gassed Schilling gets his third start of the Series. Once again he is heroic: 7.1 IP, 6 H, 2 R, 0 BB, 9 K's. Curt is named co-MVP along with teammate Randy Johnson. *Fenway Park, Game Two, 2004 World Series:* On a gimpy ankle, Curt gamely throws six innings against the St. Louis Cardinals, allows just one run, and earns the victory.

In short, Curt Schilling is one of the rare guys who can raise his game—through grit, guts, and greatness—when he stands on the biggest stage, under the brightest lights. No one ever accused him of being shy. Curt succeeds because of the exceptional command of his pitches. His control is uncanny; the ball goes where he wants it, and pretty quickly, too. Over the last four seasons, Curt has struck out 1,006 batters while walking only 139, for an otherworldly 7:1 K/BB ratio. That's a sign of one impressive hurler!

RED SOCKS

The legend of Curt Schilling grew when he pitched in Game Six of the 2004 ALCS, and again in the World Series, on a badly injured ankle.

The injury originally occured early in the regular season, but worsened in a playoff game against the Anaheim Angels. When Curt attempted to pitch in Game One of the ALCS against the Yankees, he found that he could not get his normal "push-off" from the rubber. For a power pitcher, that's trouble. His fastball, normally around 92-93 MPH, sat at a hittable 86 MPH. Schilling lasted three innings before limping off the field—done for the day, probably down for the season.

Meanwhile, Dr. Bill Morgan of the Red Sox medical staff experimented with a surgery that might keep Curt's tendon in place. He tested the procedure on a cadaver before trying it out on Curt himself. On the morning of Game Six, a must-win for the Red Sox, Curt received three sutures deep in his ankle. Only one held. For Game Two of the World Series, four sutures were used. Blood famously seeped through his sock. All of the sutures popped open.

Curt Schilling won both starts, allowing just two runs in 13 innings.

SCHILLING BY THE NUMBERS

	G	ERA	W-L	IP	H	ER	BB	SO
2001 WS	3	1.69	1-0	21.3	12	4	2	26
Career WS	6	2.11	3-1	42.7	29	10	8	39
Career Postseason	15	2.06	7-2	109.3	79	25	22	104

BOSTON TEA PARTY!

LET'S NOT KID OURSELVES. The ALCS was one of the most riveting postseason series in baseball history. The Red Sox achieved the impossible by sweeping the Yankees after losing the first three games. It was exciting, intense, stomach-churning, and absolutely brilliant baseball. In comparison, the 2004 World Series didn't stand a chance. So Beantown's Best, a rag-tag bunch of self-proclaimed "Idiots," simply set about the task of defeating a quality Cardinals team. After four solid wins, they left no doubt. **BOSTON HAD WON ITS FIRST WORLD SERIES SINCE 1918!**

27

GAME 1
Mark Bellhorn hits a two-run homer in the bottom of the 8th to put the Sox ahead to stay. A game of inches? The ball struck the right field foul pole!

STL	011 302 020	9 11 1
BOS	403 000 22x	11 13 4

ST. LOUIS CARDINALS

	AB	R	H	RBI
Renteria ss	4	1	2	1
Walker rf	5	1	4	2
Pujols 1b	3	0	0	0
Rolen 3b	5	0	0	0
Edmonds cf	4	2	1	0
Sanders dh	3	1	0	0
Womack 2b	1	1	0	0
Anderson 2b	2	0	1	0
Matheny c	2	0	1	2
Marquis pr	0	1	0	0
Molina c	1	0	0	0
Taguchi lf	3	1	1	1
Cedeno ph,lf	2	1	1	0
Williams p	0	0	0	0
Haren p	0	0	0	0
Calero p	0	0	0	0
King p	0	0	0	0
Eldred p	0	0	0	0
Tavarez p	0	0	0	0
Totals	35	9	11	6

FIELDING–E: Renteria (1).
BATTING–2B: Walker 2 (2); Renteria (1); Anderson (1). HR: Walker (1).

BOSTON RED SOX

	AB	R	H	RBI
Damon cf	6	1	2	1
Cabrera ss	4	2	1	1
Ramirez lf	5	0	3	2
Ortiz dh	3	1	2	4
Millar 1b	5	1	1	0
Mientkiewicz 1b	0	0	0	0
Nixon rf	3	0	0	0
Kapler ph,rf	1	0	0	0
Mueller 3b	3	1	1	1
Mirabelli c	3	1	1	0
Varitek ph,c	2	1	0	0
Bellhorn 2b	3	3	2	2
Reese 2b	0	0	0	0
Wakefield p	0	0	0	0
Arroyo p	0	0	0	0
Timlin p	0	0	0	0
Embree p	0	0	0	0
Foulke p	0	0	0	0
Totals	38	11	13	11

FIELDING–E: Ramirez 2 (2), Millar (1), Arroyo (1). BATTING–2B: Damon (1); Millar (1). HR: Ortiz (1); Bellhorn (1).

ST. LOUIS

	IP	H	HR	R	ER	BB	K
Williams	2.1	8	1	7	7	3	1
Haren	3.2	2	0	0	0	3	1
Calero	0.1	1	0	2	2	2	0
King	0.1	1	0	0	0	0	0
Eldred	0.1	0	0	0	0	0	1
Tavarez L(0-1)	1	1	1	2	1	0	0
Totals	8	13	2	11	10	8	3

BOSTON

	IP	H	HR	R	ER	BB	K
Wakefield	3.2	3	1	5	5	2	2
Arroyo	2.1	4	0	2	2	0	4
Timlin	1.1	1	0	1	1	0	0
Embree	0	1	0	1	0	0	0
Foulke W(1-0)	1.2	2	0	0	0	1	3
Totals	9.0	11	1	9	8	6	9

GAME 2
Behind the pitching of Curt Schilling, and two-out hits by Jason Varitek, Mark Bellhorn, and Orlando Cabrera, the Red Sox take a 2-0 Series lead.

STL	000 100 010	2 5 0
BOS	200 202 00x	6 8 4

ST. LOUIS CARDINALS

	AB	R	H	RBI
Renteria ss	3	1	0	0
Walker rf	4	0	0	0
Pujols 1b	4	1	3	0
Rolen 3b	3	0	0	1
Edmonds cf	4	0	0	0
Sanders lf	3	0	0	0
Womack 2b	4	0	1	0
Matheny c	4	0	1	0
Anderson dh	2	0	0	0
Taguchi ph,dh	1	0	0	0
Morris p	0	0	0	0
Eldred p	0	0	0	0
King p	0	0	0	0
Marquis p	0	0	0	0
Reyes p	0	0	0	0
Totals	32	2	5	1

BATTING–2B: Pujols 2 (2).

BOSTON RED SOX

	AB	R	H	RBI
Damon cf	5	1	1	0
Cabrera ss	4	0	1	2
Ramirez lf	4	1	1	0
Kapler lf	0	0	0	0
Ortiz dh	3	1	0	0
Varitek c	3	0	1	2
Millar 1b	1	1	0	0
Mientkiewicz pr,1b	0	0	0	0
Nixon rf	4	1	1	0
Mueller 3b	3	1	2	0
Bellhorn 2b	3	0	1	2
Reese 2b	1	0	0	0
Schilling p	0	0	0	0
Embree p	0	0	0	0
Timlin p	0	0	0	0
Foulke p	0	0	0	0
Totals	31	6	8	6

FIELDING–E: Mueller 3 (3), Bellhorn (1).
BATTING–2B: Mueller (1); Bellhorn (1).
3B: Varitek (1).

ST. LOUIS

	IP	H	HR	R	ER	BB	K
Morris L(0-1)	4.1	4	0	4	4	3
Eldred	1.1	4	0	2	2	0	1
King	0.1	0	0	0	0	0	1
Marquis	1	0	0	0	0	2	0
Reyes	1	0	0	0	0	0	0
Totals	8	8	0	6	6	6	5

BOSTON

	IP	H	HR	R	ER	BB	K
Schilling W(1-0)	6	4	0	1	0	1	4
Embree	1	0	0	0	0	0	3
Timlin	0.2	1	0	1	1	1	0
Foulke	1.1	0	0	0	0	0	2
Totals	9	5	0	2	1	2	9

GAME 3
Manny Ramirez hits a homer and throws out a Cardinal at the plate—all in the first inning. Pedro Martinez throws seven innings of three-hit ball.

BOS	100 120 000	4 9 0
STL	000 000 001	1 4 0

BOSTON RED SOX

	AB	R	H	RBI
Damon cf	5	1	1	0
Cabrera ss	4	1	2	0
Ramirez lf	4	1	2	2
Ortiz 1b	4	0	1	0
Mientkiewicz 1b	0	0	0	0
Varitek c	3	0	0	0
Mueller 3b	4	1	2	1
Nixon rf	3	0	1	1
Kapler ph,rf	1	0	0	0
Bellhorn 2b	3	0	0	0
Reese 2b	0	0	0	0
Martinez p	2	0	0	0
Millar ph	1	0	0	0
Timlin p	0	0	0	0
Foulke p	0	0	0	0
Totals	34	4	9	4

BATTING–2B: Mueller (2); Damon (2); Cabrera (1). HR: Ramirez (1).

ST. LOUIS CARDINALS

	AB	R	H	RBI
Renteria ss	4	0	1	0
Walker rf	3	1	1	1
Pujols 1b	4	0	1	0
Rolen 3b	3	0	0	0
Edmonds cf	3	0	0	0
Sanders lf	3	0	0	0
Womack 2b	3	0	0	0
Matheny c	2	0	0	0
Cedeno ph	1	0	0	0
Tavarez p	0	0	0	0
Suppan p	1	0	1	0
Reyes p	0	0	0	0
Anderson ph	1	0	0	0
Calero p	0	0	0	0
King p	0	0	0	0
Mabry ph	1	0	0	0
Molina c	0	0	0	0
Totals	29	1	4	1

BATTING - 2B: Renteria (2). HR: Walker (2).

BOSTON

	IP	H	HR	R	ER	BB	K
Martinez W(1-0)	7	3	0	0	0	2	6
Timlin	1	0	0	0	0	0	0
Foulke	1	1	1	1	1	0	2
Totals	9	4	1	1	1	2	8

ST. LOUIS

	IP	H	HR	R	ER	BB	K
Suppan L(0-1)	4.2	8	1	4	4	1	4
Reyes	0.1	0	0	0	0	0	0
Calero	1	1	0	0	0	2	0
King	2	0	0	0	0	1	0
Tavarez	1	0	0	0	0	0	1
Totals	9	9	1	4	4	4	5

GAME 4 It is Derek Lowe's turn to toss a three-hit gem, as again the Red Sox silence the famed Card attack. Johnny Damon leads off with a home run. Trot Nixon delivers three doubles, drives in two. Sweep!

BOS	102 000 000	3	9	0
STL	000 000 000	0	4	0

BOSTON RED SOX

	AB	R	H	RBI
Damon cf	5	1	2	1
Cabrera ss	5	0	0	0
Ramirez lf	4	0	1	0
Ortiz 1b	3	1	1	0
Mientkiewicz 1b	1	0	0	0
Varitek c	5	1	1	0
Mueller 3b	4	0	1	0
Nixon rf	4	0	3	2
Kapler pr,rf	0	0	0	0
Bellhorn 2b	1	0	0	0
Reese pr,2b	0	0	0	0
Lowe p	2	0	0	0
Millar ph	1	0	0	0
Arroyo p	0	0	0	0
Embree p	0	0	0	0
Foulke p	0	0	0	0
Totals	35	3	9	3

BATTING - 2B: Nixon 3 (3); Ortiz (1).
3B: Damon (1). HR: Damon (1).

ST. LOUIS CARDINALS

	AB	R	H	RBI
Womack 2b	3	0	1	0
Luna ph,2b	1	0	0	0
Walker rf	2	0	0	0
Pujols 1b	4	0	1	0
Rolen 3b	4	0	0	0
Edmonds cf	4	0	0	0
Renteria ss	4	0	2	0
Mabry lf	3	0	0	0
Isringhausen p	0	0	0	0
Molina c	2	0	0	0
Cedeno ph	1	0	0	0
Matheny c	0	0	0	0
Marquis p	1	0	0	0
Anderson ph	1	0	0	0
Haren p	0	0	0	0
Sanders lf	0	0	0	0
Totals	30	0	4	0

BATTING - 2B: Renteria (3).

BOSTON	IP	H	HR	R	ER	BB	K
Lowe W(1-0)	7	3	0	0	0	1	4
Arroyo	0.1	0	0	0	0	1	0
Embree	0.2	0	0	0	0	0	1
Foulke SV(1)	1	1	0	0	0	0	1
Totals	9	4	0	0	0	2	6

ST. LOUIS							
Marquis L(0-1)	6	6	1	3	3	5	4
Haren	1	2	0	0	0	0	1
Isringhausen	2	1	0	0	0	1	2
Totals	9	9	1	3	3	6	7

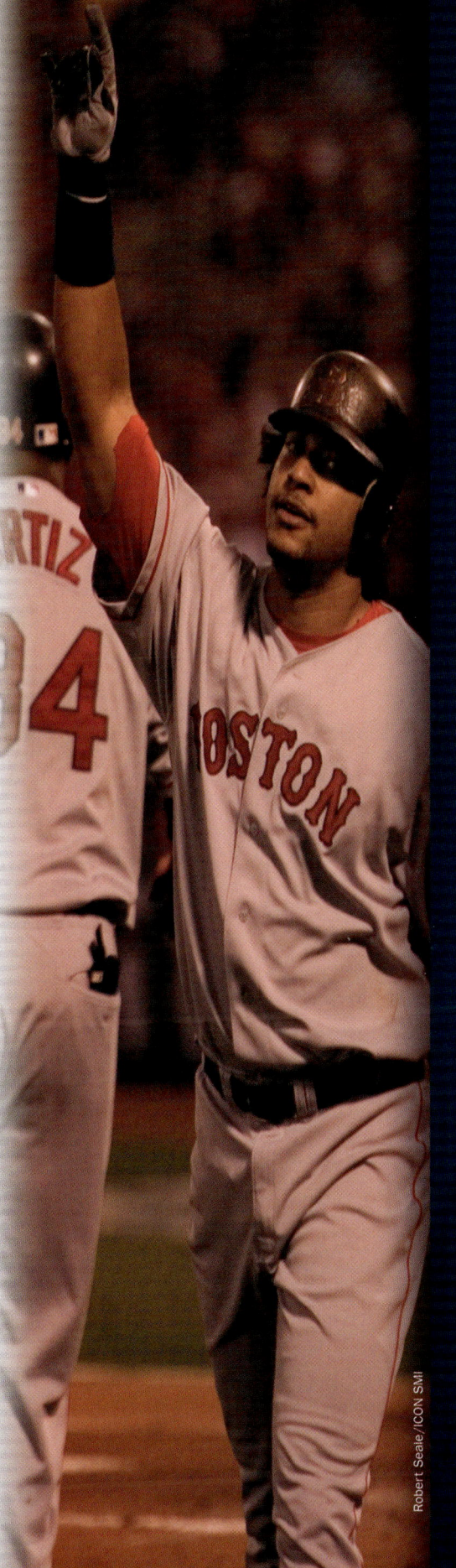

THE CURSE OF THE BAMBINO

The Boston Red Sox were once baseball's winningest franchise. One of their greatest players was Babe Ruth, a top pitcher who converted to the outfield. In 1919, his last season with the Red Sox, Babe hit .322 and set a record by smashing 29 home runs. In January of 1920, Boston owner Harry Frazee sold Ruth to the New York Yankees. Since that infamous date, the Red Sox had appeared in four World Series—losing each one in Game 7. Many fans blamed it on "The Curse of the Bambino."

RED SOX WORLD SERIES HISTORY

1903 Red Sox beat the Pirates to win the first World Series ever played.

1912 Red Sox defeat Christy Mathewson and the New York Giants.

1914 Red Sox defeat Connie Mack's Philadelphia A's.

1915 Red Sox prevail over Philadelphia again.

1916 Behind the pitching of young lefthander Babe Ruth, the Red Sox defeat the Brooklyn Dodgers.

1918 Red Sox triumph over the Chicago Cubs to win their 6th World Series. It would be a looooong wait for another.

1946 Red Sox lose in seven games to the St. Louis Cardinals.

1967 Red Sox lose in seven games to the St. Louis Cardinals. Again!

1975 Red Sox lose in seven games to the Cincinnati Reds.

1986 Red Sox lose in seven games to the New York Mets.

2004 Red Sox sweep the St. Louis Cardinals. Finally!

WORLD SERIES
STATS & FACTS

HITTING LEADERS
SINGLE SERIES:

BATTING AVERAGE
Billy Hatcher	.750	1990 WS
Babe Ruth	.625	1928 WS
Ricky Ledee	.600	1998 WS

ON-BASE %
Billy Hatcher	.800	1990 WS
Lou Gehrig	.706	1928 WS
Barry Bonds	.700	2002 WS

SLUGGING %
Lou Gehrig	1.727	1928 WS
Babe Ruth	1.375	1928 WS
Barry Bonds	1.294	2002 WS

AT BATS
Jimmy Collins	36	1903 WS
Ginger Beaumont	34	1903 WS
Fred Clarke	34	1903 WS

RUNS SCORED
Reggie Jackson	10	1977 WS
Paul Molitor	10	1993 WS
Lenny Dykstra	9	1993 WS
Lou Gehrig	9	1932 WS
Babe Ruth	9	1928 WS
Roy White	9	1978 WS

HITS
Marty Barrett	13	1986 WS
Lou Brock	13	1968 WS
Bobby Richardson	13	1964 WS

TOTAL BASES
Reggie Jackson	25	1977 WS
Willie Stargell	25	1979 WS
Lou Brock	24	1968 WS
Paul Molitor	24	1993 WS
Duke Snider	24	1952 WS

HOME RUNS
Reggie Jackson	5	1977 WS
Willie Aikens	4	1980 WS
Hank Bauer	4	1958 WS
Barry Bonds	4	2002 WS
Lenny Dykstra	4	1993 WS
Lou Gehrig	4	1928 WS
Babe Ruth	4	1926 WS
Duke Snider	4	1952 WS
Duke Snider	4	1955 WS
Gene Tenace	4	1972 WS

RBI
Bobby Richardson	12	1960 WS
Mickey Mantle	11	1960 WS
Sandy Alomar	10	1997 WS
Yogi Berra	10	1956 WS
Ted Kluszewski	10	1959 WS

BASES ON BALLS
Barry Bonds	13	2002 WS
Babe Ruth	11	1926 WS
Gene Tenace	11	1973 WS

STOLEN BASES
Lou Brock	7	1967 WS
Lou Brock	7	1968 WS
Vince Coleman	6	1987 WS
Kenny Lofton	6	1995 WS
Honus Wagner	6	1909 WS

TIMES ON BASE
Barry Bonds	21	2002 WS
Marty Barrett	18	1986 WS
Mickey Mantle	18	1960 WS

CAREER:
(minimum 30 plate appearances)

BATTING AVERAGE
Dave Robertson	.500
Vic Wertz	.500
Barry Bonds	.471

ON-BASE %
Barry Bonds	.700
Al Weis	.562
Vic Wertz	.556

SLUGGING %
Barry Bonds	1.294
Vic Wertz	.938
Ted Kluszewski	.826

WORLD SERIES
STATS & FACTS

GAMES
Yogi Berra	150
Mickey Mantle	130
Elston Howard	108

RUNS
Mickey Mantle	84
Yogi Berra	82
Babe Ruth	74

HITS
Yogi Berra	142
Mickey Mantle	118
Frankie Frisch	116

TOTAL BASES
Mickey Mantle	246
Yogi Berra	234
Babe Ruth	192

HOME RUNS
Mickey Mantle	36
Babe Ruth	30
Yogi Berra	24

RBI
Mickey Mantle	80
Yogi Berra	78
Lou Gehrig	70

BASES ON BALLS
Mickey Mantle	86
Babe Ruth	66
Yogi Berra	64

STOLEN BASES
Lou Brock	28
Eddie Collins	28
Frank Chance	20
Phil Rizzuto	20

PITCHING LEADERS
SINGLE SERIES:

GAMES
Darold Knowles	7	1973 WS
Pedro Borbon	6	1972 WS
Hugh Casey	6	1947 WS
Rollie Fingers	6	1972 WS
Rollie Fingers	6	1973 WS
Dan Quisenberry	6	1980 WS
Felix Rodriguez	6	2002 WS
Tim Worrell	6	2002 WS

SAVES
John Wetteland	4	1996 WS
Roy Face	3	1960 WS
Troy Percival	3	2002 WS
Mariano Rivera	3	1998 WS
Kent Tekulve	3	1979 WS

STRIKEOUTS
Bob Gibson	35	1968 WS
Bob Gibson	31	1964 WS
Sandy Koufax	29	1965 WS

CAREER:
(minimum 20 innings pitched)

ERA
Jack Billingham	0.36
Harry Brecheen	0.83
Claude Osteen	0.86

WINS
Whitey Ford	10
Bob Gibson	7
Allie Reynolds	7
Red Ruffing	7

GAMES
Whitey Ford	22
Mariano Rivera	20
Mike Stanton	20

SAVES
Mariano Rivera	9
Rollie Fingers	6
Johnny Murphy	4
Robb Nen	4
Allie Reynolds	4
John Wetteland	4

INNINGS
Whitey Ford	146.0
Christy Mathewson	101.2
Red Ruffing	85.2

STRIKEOUTS
Whitey Ford	94
Bob Gibson	92
Allie Reynolds	62

WORLD SERIES
MVP AWARD WINNERS

2004	Manny Ramirez		**1980**	Mike Schmidt
2003	Josh Beckett		**1979**	Willie Stargell
2002	Troy Glaus		**1978**	Bucky Dent
2001	Randy Johnson		**1977**	Reggie Jackson
	Curt Schilling		**1976**	Johnny Bench
2000	Derek Jeter		**1975**	Pete Rose
1999	Mariano Rivera		**1974**	Rollie Fingers
1998	Scott Brosius		**1973**	Reggie Jackson
1997	Livan Hernandez		**1972**	Gene Tenace
1996	John Wetteland		**1971**	Roberto Clemente
1995	Tom Glavine		**1970**	Brooks Robinson
1994	*Series Cancelled*		**1969**	Donn Clendenon
1993	Paul Molitor		**1968**	Mickey Lolich
1992	Pat Borders		**1967**	Bob Gibson
1991	Jack Morris		**1966**	Frank Robinson
1990	Jose Rijo		**1965**	Sandy Koufax
1989	Dave Stewart		**1964**	Bob Gibson
1988	Orel Hershiser		**1963**	Sandy Koufax
1987	Frank Viola		**1962**	Ralph Terry
1986	Ray Knight		**1961**	Whitey Ford
1985	Bret Saberhagen		**1960**	Bobby Richardson
1984	Alan Trammell		**1959**	Larry Sherry
1983	Rick Dempsey		**1958**	Bob Turley
1982	Darrell Porter		**1957**	Lew Burdette
1981	Ron Cey		**1956**	Don Larsen
	Pedro Guerrero		**1955**	Johnny Podres
	Steve Yeager			